MW01272942

Giving It & Taking It

John W. Alexander &
Stephen A. Hayner

InterVarsity Press
P.O. Box 1400, Downers Grove, IL 60515
World Wide Web: www.ivpress.com
E-mail: mail@ivpress.com

InterVarsity Press® is the book-publishing division of InterVarsity Christian Fellowship/USA®, a student movement active on campus at hundreds of universities, colleges and schools of nursing in the United States of America, and a member movement of the International Fellowship of Evangelical Students. For information about local and regional activities, write Public Relations Dept., InterVarsity Christian Fellowship/USA, 6400 Schroeder Rd., P.O. Box 7895, Madison, WI 53707-7895.

Personal references in the text refer to John W. Alexander.

ISBN 0-87784-057-1

Printed in the United States of America ∞

15	14	13	12	11	10	9	8	7	6	5	4	3	2	1
11	10	09	08	07	06	05	04	03	02	01	00			

You're troubled by a problem with your neighbors. They're nice and you know they mean well, but they really are hard to get along with. They're noisy. Their yard is a mess. Any way you look at it, things could be much better.

Or you have a youth minister, Bill, who just isn't listening to the kids. The teens would like to have a hand in what's going on, but Bill decides everything. If you confront him, he'll think you're trying to run the program. Moreover, Bill has a very short fuse.

Or you've been on the receiving end of some pretty hard words from your friends— at least you *thought* they were your friends!

Lately they've been getting after you for everything. It seems as if all they do is criticize. And it's getting awfully hard to take.

Criticism can be a helpful form of communication. But it can feel like one of the worst. A mature pastor commented recently:

> The thing that gets me down is the criticism people keep expressing toward me and my work. It ranges from complaints about the colors I wear on Sunday to the quality of my singing to my conversational style—even assertions that I am arrogant, dominant or ignorant about ministry. The criticism comes in the form of letters, e-mail messages, notes on the comment column of our attendance record, voice mail and direct remarks. It doesn't come from our leadership (thank God) but from other folk who seem to be carrying tremendous anger and unhappiness. Both men and women do this, people of different ages. . . . There doesn't seem to be one identifiable demographic "group." So believing this is an important growth point, I want to know how to handle it. I take things personally

and am constantly fighting the temptation to view these few people as representatives of the whole congregation.

By a dictionary definition *criticism* can be either positive or negative. Most of us when we hear the word immediately assume something harsh. Consider, however, that movie critics may speak glowingly or disparagingly of a film. Criticism—critique, evaluation or analysis—can be positive when someone identifies strengths, accomplishments and other good points. Positive criticism identifies satisfactory achievement as determined by those making the judgment.

We all need that kind of criticism! It is essential for a healthy self-image and for perseverance in good works. A good parent, teacher, pastor or leader motivates people by building their confidence and by expressing appreciation for not only their finished products but also their effort and willingness to try.

Failing to express positive evaluation is a weakness of many individuals and groups. Some supervisors, for example, seem incapable of giving compliments, as though they expect everyone to do their best without anyone noticing or expressing thanks in return. But without genuine appreciation or commendation people feel taken for granted, which leads to resentment. Then negative criticism, which must inevitably come in any healthy relationship, will have an especially nasty bite.

Our pastor friend has a number of very specific questions regarding negative criticism:

How do you answer criticism without "being defensive"? I want to learn. I don't want to be insensitive or arrogant. Am I? Or is it just their problem and I have to let it go? When a truckload of criticism gets dumped on me fifteen minutes before a worship service begins, what can I do to get back on track? I'm just wiped out by it. Or when I receive a critical letter, do I answer it? Is there ever a point where it's no longer helpful to answer another letter from the same person?

Negative Criticism

We all feel the sting when someone points out our weaknesses, mistakes or flaws. At minimum such negative evaluation indicates unsatisfactory performance, but if you are like most people you often take it as a devaluation of your very self.

Such criticism, however, does not have to be destructive. We can learn to accept negative feedback in a way that does not require our becoming defensive, resentful or unmotivated. And we can learn to evaluate unsatisfactory performance in others in ways that sustain their dignity, help them to grow and even strengthen our mutual relationship. "Iron sharpens iron, and one person sharpens the wits of another" (Prov 27:17).

When based on true evidence and expressed in a loving manner to the proper people, negative criticism can help a person or a group recognize errors of judgment and begin to change. We cannot overcome weaknesses of which we are ignorant or avoid mistakes that we do not anticipate. Negative

7

criticism can be the surgeon's knife that cuts away a cancer in our lives and makes way for wholeness once again.

Leaders must pay attention to the dynamics of negative criticism because of its terribly destructive potential. Its effects are compounded when based on hearsay or subjective evidence, when facts are improperly analyzed or when the criticism is communicated in an unloving way or for the wrong motives.

Criticism can turn people against each other and destroy fellowship. Criticism is like fire: in the right place and the right time and under control, it can do much good. But in the wrong place, at the wrong time and raging out of control, it can wreak enormous damage.

Three forms of criticism are especially hurtful.

Gossip is a form of slander and is a common mode of negative criticism. Christians are not immune. Out of legitimate concern for others we often fall into the trap of speaking about people behind their backs.

Sometimes we call it "sharing prayer requests." This sort of slander sows suspicion and discord (Prov 6:19). Gossip is a triple-action poison. Our gossip affects both ourselves and our listeners, but it also damages the reputation of the people about whom we gossip.

Gossip is often about power. Saying "I know something that you don't know" is a pernicious way of trying to diminish someone else by elevating ourselves. Or we might use gossip to vent our frustrations when we are too frightened to risk criticizing someone in a higher position. But the fact that appropriate direct criticism is difficult does not make gossip any more acceptable.

James 3:5-8 warns us of the power of the tongue, and Psalm 15:2-3 admonishes us to walk blamelessly, speak truth from the heart and avoid slander with the tongue. With such straightforward teaching on the matter from Scripture, we must not be naive about the dangers of gossip or careless with what we think is benign conversation about others.

Confrontation, when used as a means of delivering negative criticism, often produces problems rather than results. It is the opposite of gossip in that the critic goes directly to a person or group, but it expresses negative criticism in a loveless manner. Confrontation is often disguised as being an honest encounter—"just telling the truth."

The problem with such criticism is that people who confront others often believe they have all the facts before they ever go to see the person. Our goal must never be to "tell them off" rather than to resolve an issue. If we accuse without carefully measuring our words and attitudes, even the valid points of our criticism will be damaging rather than constructive.

It is true that followers of Christ see the effects of sin in the world, perhaps more clearly than other people do, but we are called to "build one another up," not to tear each other down.

Public complaint is actually a form of gossip, but since it has become so rampant and is so difficult to stop or defend against, it must be treated separately. Public complaint is the practice of publishing hurtful material or broadcasting accusations through radio, the Internet or faxes without consulting the person or organization being targeted. Unlike gossip, which tends to breed suspicion through the grapevine, public complaint is perpetrated through newsletters, talk shows and chat rooms where accusations are laid out for all to see. This kind of faultfinding is a form of baiting, demanding that the accused parties defend themselves publicly against charges that have never been established.

Diana Owen, professor of government at Georgetown University, says that this "talk radio" kind of discourse vents pent-up anger, cynicism and confrontation in an irresponsible way. People "feel a part of a community, participate in it, and yet do so anonymously and without obligation." They can launch venomous personal attacks without the responsibility of owning up to them. A similar anonymity encourages the mean-spirited messages that pervade Internet forums, where participants are routinely "flamed."[1]

And so the question: How do we deal with negative criticism? Is there a way to control this fire so that it produces benefits instead of damage? The answer surely is not excessive positive criticism. None of us needs flattery. Nor can the solution be the absence of negative evaluation. We need that; how else can we become aware of our weaknesses? Therefore let us consider suggestions for giving and receiving criticism in a constructive way.

Five Ways to Give Constructive Criticism

Bishop Stephen Neill, in his study of the fruit of the Spirit, "The Difference in Being a Christian," defines *love* as "the steady direction of the will toward another's lasting good."[2] Love is obedience in action, specific service to another person no matter how we feel about them. If we are sincere in our concern for those we must criticize and resolved to work for their good, we will offer criticism that is truly constructive. Here are some steps for expressing constructive criticism even when it may be negative.

1. *Pray.* Take time to pray before approaching anyone with a negative (or positive) evaluation. First, be certain of your own motives. Ask yourself and the Lord, *Why am I expressing this criticism? Has my ego been hurt so that I want to embarrass somebody else? Or is my concern truly to help this person [or group]?*

Consider also how your criticism will be viewed. Listeners will be more attentive to your evaluations if they respect you. There is only one way to earn that respect: through a record of servanthood and deeds well done. This is why it is risky in new relationships to come on strong with negative criticism. This doesn't mean that you must remain silent until you become well accepted, but it does mean that you have work to do before your criticism will be taken seriously.

Taking your judgments first into the presence of God can clarify a lot. Then if you do approach someone with criticism, ask God to make it truly constructive.

2. Go directly and privately. Jesus urged, "If another member of the church sins against you, go and point out the fault when the two of you are alone" (Mt 18:15). This is a great principle whether you are facing your parents or your child, your pastor or friend, your teacher or pupil, your supervisor or subordinate. Criticizing someone in the presence of others prior to discussing the matter privately is a violation of 1 Corinthians 13:4: "Love is kind."

I once encountered a man who had heard via the grapevine that I had said something of which he disapproved. He confronted me in a public meeting: "There's something that has been sticking in my craw for almost a year." He went on to detail what he had heard and how it had offended him. He did not inquire whether I actually had said it (I had not) or whether I might have been misunderstood. It was an unpleasant situation both because he did not have the facts straight and because he embarrassed himself and the whole group.

A key principle is that criticism should be communicated in the most personal way appropriate. A face-to-face encounter, when possible, is usually best. In a strained personal relationship, speaking face to face may either (1) cause the critic's courage to evaporate or (2) make the receiver tense and defensive, and thus unable truly to hear. Writing can be a good medium for offering the criticism, provided that words are carefully and accurately chosen and that the tone is not one of unrelenting anger. Words on paper can shout just as loudly as a voice.

Because some people may come across as either overbearing or timid, it may be necessary to find a respected third party to help. An intermediary may convey the criticism in the critic's place or may accompany the person needing some emotional support. Such a procedure is not as satisfactory as direct one-to-one communication, but it is better than airing a complaint through gossip or allowing it to turn into a root of bitterness.

3. Lead with positive questions. Give the other person the benefit of the doubt; offer a chance to clarify or explain rather than asking a question that assumes certain things and makes an accusation. Confrontational or loaded questions will not create a climate suitable for resolving issues. A colleague once approached me privately over breakfast and in a nonthreatening manner said, "I heard a report of something you said, but it doesn't sound like you. Did you really say this? If so, please help me understand why." I appreciated this colleague's positive approach and was more than happy to oblige.

There are practical reasons for leading with positive questions. The most important reason is that the person being criticized may have information that you do not. By asking questions first, you can clear up the matter before further misunderstandings occur. Asking questions also allows you to get at the principal issue—by listening first and not attacking

But suppose the one being criticized is not free to divulge information. Maybe the issue revolves around a personal issue, and confidences need to be kept for the sake of the others involved. At such times the problem boils down to a question of trust. If you trust your colleague, your friend, your teacher—the one you respect enough to confront—you will accept the limits and continue your respect and friendship rather than turn away.

4. Be honest and specific. It does no good to go to all the trouble of meeting personally and getting the correct information if you then deal in vague generalities or speak less than the truth. So agree from the beginning that you will communicate, both verbally and nonverbally, what you honestly think and feel—and why. Support your criticism with objective evidence rather than subjective opinions. The term *objective* refers to evidence that anybody could observe, evidence that is the same no matter who views it and therefore not dependent on the viewer's prejudice. That will mean first procuring adequate data so that you know what you are talking about. A lot of negative criticism flows from people who are simply unfamiliar with the facts and so resort to impugning other people's motives or venting their own opinions.

Objective evidence is specific. It deals with actual behavior. Are you dissatisfied with the growth rate in your church group? Procure objective information about the actual numbers that substantiate the rate of growth—or decline—and then indicate what you think constitutes satisfactory growth. Do you dislike the music in your group? If so, do some research on music options, then confer with those responsible for the music and explain why you are dissatisfied. Criticism cast in terms of your own personal feelings helps only if it sets the stage for more objective evaluation.

5. *Suggest alternatives.* Michelangelo, in re-sponse to a fellow artist who was very critical of another person's work, is reported to have said to the artist, "Criticize by creating!" Anybody can point out weaknesses; it takes creativity to propose solutions. It is a sign of immaturity to blame someone for a problem but not suggest ways to solve it or offer to help find a solution. A useful approach is to consider suggestions along these lines:

"Here's what I think you should stop doing."

"Here's what I think you should start doing."

"Here's what I think you should continue doing, but I believe it would be better if you did it this way."

You may not be able to give either practical suggestions or active assistance right away. So offer to pray for the person and for the situation that needs to change. Then volunteer at least a little help, even if it is only to think further about the responses you received to your questions and offer specific observations and suggestions later. Balance your criticism with an initiative to become part of the solution.

Our nation is riddled with angry people who make every effort to point out what is wrong but who seem incapable of offering one word to make things better. Rare indeed is the individual who can temper an indictment with a commensurate dose of viable options. The criticism that followers of Jesus offer can differ from this destructive pattern. Both the substance and the tone of our criticism will be distinctive. As Eugene Peterson so well contemporizes 1 Corinthians 13:6-7 in *The Message,* the Christian's love "takes pleasure in the flowering of truth, puts up with anything, trusts God always, always looks for the best."

On the Receiving End
If you are a leader, you will certainly experience criticism. By virtue of your position or your influence you will make decisions that

affect other people. Some people will not like those decisions, and they will let you know it. Working with good people or in an overtly faith-based organization is no protection. How then do you deal with it?

A key characteristic of effective leaders is teachability. Therefore one extreme to avoid is to ignore criticism. I once asked a chief executive officer how he dealt with critical letters. He answered, "I simply throw them in the wastebasket." By doing this he missed valuable input for his leadership. His board of trustees fired him after a relatively brief tenure; his refusal to learn from criticism was one factor in his undoing.

At the other extreme is the supersensitive response of paying too much attention to criticism. Overreacting to negative input is a sign of insecurity, and it can affect one's emotional health. On one occasion I spoke tactfully to a colleague about a way to improve our work together. But the response was surprising. After hearing the criticism and suggestions for change, the person responded, "Do you want me to resign?" To the contrary, the point of the conversation was to figure out how we could continue to work together in a better way. But this person lived in such fear of criticism that any suggestion was taken as a threat.

Many people work or live in environments that foster such insecurity. Workplaces, schools and families that tolerate gossip, secrecy and public put-downs create a climate where people feel unappreciated and treated with a lack of respect. Fear becomes a dominant factor. In that kind of atmosphere, it is no wonder that criticism is interpreted as a personal affront rather than an effort to edify. To transform such an environment we must ourselves be open to criticism and able to respond positively. We must learn to foster an atmosphere of grace.

Five Ways to Receive Criticism

Receiving a negative critique is not pleasant. But you can survive the experience and actually benefit from it if you assume the same motivation of love considered earlier. The goal is not to defend yourself or to create divisions. Rather we as Christians are to "lead a life worthy of the calling to which [we] have been called, with all humility and gentleness, with patience, bearing with one another in love, making every effort to maintain the unity of the Spirit in the bond of peace" (Eph 4:1-3).

Here are a few self-disciplines that will help you hear criticism constructively.

1. Pray and be patient. Ask the Lord to guide you in responding to the criticism. Ask God to make you sensitive to hear what should be heard, strong to disregard what is inappropriate, and able to control temper and anger. Recognize that in every criticism there is at least a kernel of truth, and pray for the wisdom to discern that kernel.

The natural reaction to criticism is to fight back with defensive tactics, explanations and excuses. Anxiety peaks sharply when criticism hits home. It is as if a tightly coiled spring deep inside is cocked to snap back in self-defense. So we must ask the Lord for patience and enough self-assurance not to become defensive.

2. Let the critic finish. If you are being criticized face-to-face or over the telephone, let the critic finish. Don't interrupt. Interruptions choke off the message and deny you the whole story. They can also raise the emotive level of the one who is criticizing so that he or she pushes all the more strongly. When the critic appears to be through, encourage him or her to go on. If you are conversing in person, look the other in the eye and ask, "Is there more?" Indicate that you desire to hear everything, that the critic shouldn't hold back at this point. In other words, *listen.* Give your critic your undivided attention.

If you have the time, give a response then and there. Otherwise ask if you could meet again, on neutral turf—have a meal together or go for a walk—to discuss the problem. Activities such as these keep difficult encounters from becoming too tense.

3. Give careful consideration to the evidence. You may discover that the evidence for the criticism is valid. If the evidence is adequate and the conclusions are appropriate, then your critic has done you a great favor. This is true even if the manner in which the message has been delivered is less than helpful. The person may have called your attention to a weakness that you knew nothing about, to a mistake that you did not realize had occurred, to oversights of which you were unaware, to consequences of decisions that you had not fully considered. "Why didn't somebody tell me?" we often ask. The critic may be endeavoring to do just that.

If the criticism comes via letter, fax or e-mail, acknowledge its receipt even if you can't respond in detail immediately. Thank the writer for taking the time to communicate and for caring enough about the integrity of the organization or ministry to be frank. Then give some indication of when you think you can get back with a more complete response.

When you do answer, remember that *letters don't smile.* Guard carefully your words and phrases. If the letter you received bristled with hostility, you may be tempted to respond in kind. If you find anger invading your re-sponse, give your feelings full expression but then throw your letter into the wastebasket. Or let it cool for twenty-four hours and then have a friend read it and give you suggestions for improving it.

If the criticism strikes you as being severe, however, it is often better not to respond in writing. Pick up the phone and let the author hear your voice. You may be surprised at how during phone conversations the apparent venom of a confrontational letter can disappear. Sometimes words used in writing come across as far more intense than intended. Ask if it would be possible to meet together to discuss the problem in person.

4. Determine the real problem. Is the criticism a baseless rumor that will die of its own accord if addressed with correct information? Does the expressed criticism indicate the basic problem, or is it only a surface issue that points to a more important issue that needs to be dealt with? Put the criticism inside the largest frame you can deal with. Look for hidden factors, and help the critic see the larger issues that may be involved.

It may be that a confrontation really represents a cry for help. Some people seem to be able to deal with their own issues only as they level criticism at others. Much criticism is "delivered to the wrong box" because a person in pain cannot or does not know how to vent emotions appropriately. If you are on the receiving end of such an attack, you will need special discernment to separate the criticism from the person's own issues, avoid becoming defensive and be truly sensitive to the critic's need.

One of the debilitating aspects of criticism, whether deserved or not, is the energy it saps from the person being criticized. To see the issues clearly you may need to get help from other people. Talk first to God, then to trusted friends. Seek advice from those whose wisdom and perspective can augment your own. People who know the other person as well as the issues involved may give you helpful insights. But sometimes, in fairness to the other person, you should refrain from talking with mutual friends. Be careful not to fall into gossip. If your friends understand enough to offer suggestions, so much the better. But even if they offer nothing in response, the very fact that they listen helps you carry the burden.

5. *Let the criticism be a source of learning.* Ask yourself, *What is the Lord trying to communicate to me via this confrontation?* Even if they appear to be "flaming," read angry letters carefully to discern whether they contain at least a germ of helpful criticism. A friend suggested that the way he inwardly responds to criticism is with the question *Is that all they could think of?* Knowing of the human propensity to sin, he realizes that there is much more that a critic could point

out. This realization helps him put a particular complaint in better perspective.

Robert O. Shaffer says in *The Management Psychologist:*

> Constructive criticism is an invaluable source of information for those who accept it. Quite often we spend more time justifying, excusing, or rationalizing an error than in trying to understand and benefit from criticism. When we are non-defensive we become aware that constructive criticism is a real compliment to us. The person offering it runs the risk of arousing our enmity, but s/he cares enough for our welfare to take the chance.[3]

A Final Word

In the end the only judge who truly matters is God himself. We must finally learn to live our lives before an audience of one. Paul says in 1 Corinthians 4:2-4:

> Moreover, it is required of stewards that they be found trustworthy. But with me it is a very small thing that I should be

judged by you or by any human court. I do not even judge myself. I am not aware of anything against myself, but I am not thereby acquitted. It is the Lord who judges me.

God's desire for us—and God's commitment to us—is that we will be transformed through the work of the Holy Spirit and by the vehicle of life's experiences into the likeness of Jesus. People will participate in that process through their criticism of us—sometimes delivered with great love, grace and care, and sometimes ineptly, ungraciously and harshly. Our task is to take it all to the Father who loves us fully, completely and with thorough understanding, and to let God sort out the criticism and use it to his glory in our lives.

Questions for Reflection or Discussion

On Criticism
1. How do you define *criticism*? How is it defined in this booklet?

30

2. Look up the following biblical passages and consider what they teach about negative criticism.

Numbers 12:1-16   Matthew 18:15-17
Numbers 14:36   Philippians 2:14
Numbers 16:1-3   Hebrews 12:15
Proverbs 6:16, 19   James 3:6-12
Proverbs 16:28

3. Think about such biblical characters as Moses, David, Jeremiah, Paul and Jesus. What passages or stories come to mind about how they criticized others or were themselves criticized? What was the response?

4. Why is criticism important to personal growth?

On Criticizing Others

1. Can you think of a time when you had to "hold a mirror" up to another person? What was the outcome of this experience? What did you learn?

2. Review the suggestions for giving criticism. Which ones are easiest for you to re-member and to practice? Which are more difficult?

You may want to choose a situation in your life where you feel that some or all of these suggestions need to be implemented, and then re-solve to follow through on them. Select a prayer partner who will hold you accountable in the matter. Choose a day to phone one another to find out what happened as you put these principles into practice.

On Being Criticized
1. What does it mean to say there is a kernel of truth in every criticism?
2. Why is it hard to listen without interrupting when someone is criticizing you? Why is it so important that you listen patiently?
3. Describe a time when someone held a mirror up to you. In what ways was it hard? Can you think of a time when it helped to change your life for the better? What helped you push through the pain of criticism to personal growth?

Notes

[1]Diana Owen, "Talk Radio's Price: A Culture of Complaint," *The Christian Science Monitor,* November 18, 1998, p. 13.
[2]Stephen Neill, "The Difference in Being a Christian," unpublished writings.
[3]Robert O. Shaffer, "The Management Psychologist," *You Are What You Do* 3, no. 3 (1966): 6-7.